STARBOUND
and other poems

by
John Enright

Copyright © 1995 by John Enright

ISBN 978-0-557-01831-4

Originally published by Axton Publishing

This Enright House edition published through Lulu.com

Other books by John Enright:

    More Fire And Other Poems

    Unholy Quest (novel)

*I'd like to offer special thanks
to Linda Tania Abrams and Debra E. Cermele,
through whose unstinting zeal
this volume joins the ranks of books in print.*

*Thanks also go to Carol Low,
to Stephanie and Joe Dejan,
and to all my other friends
at Nomos magazine,
where many of these poems
first found a home.*

Contents

Poems 1970 – 1973

Love Poems 1973 – 1974

Poems 1974 – 1977

More Poems 1978 – 1995

Poems
1970 – 1973

Enright

EMILY DICKINSON

Before your form
Of gossamer,
God shrank –
Became a fly.

Revelation
But his buzzing
In the background
Of your music.

You fingered
The strings
And in
Your webs

Tangled
Omnipotence
Danced for you
Puppetlike.

ARS POETICA

My verse, you say,
It is too light?
Ah! Curse the day
For being bright!
In these dark and heavy times
The Muse has use for clever rhymes and verse;
"Better write it light than darkness curse," as she has said.
And who exclaims "This is too light!"
Reveals his longing for the night.
I ask all such to shut quite tight their eyes;
And if they'd shut their mouths as well, as well they might,
It would be a pleasant surprise.

THE LATEST WORD FROM THE KINGDOM OF THE BLIND
(in parody of a certain college teacher)

Such ignorant and narcissistic youths
As you
    oughtn't contradict
The curious truths
I've handpicked
For your enlightenment.

When you are blessed with arrogance of years,
Having lost since
All intelligence
(not to mention eyes and ears)
I'll listen to your argument.

NOT GUILTY (after Capuletti's painting)

Beneath a sky of crystal blue swept clear,
Wearing no clothes,
Worn by no fear,
The dancer takes a pose.

Across the sparkling depths
She casts her eyes
To where the naked granite towers rise –
And prevail.
Which, like her, have never wept –
Nor shall.

ARRIVAL IN AMERICA

Not knowing all the words for what she feels,
She doesn't worry. Words and knowledge will come.
In time, she thinks, in time. For now she reels,
Giddy with breaths of free air, gazing up at the blue dome
Of sky and the towers that scrape it. "What
Evil could lurk here?" she asks. "I can't imagine any.
And even if there were, my bonds are cut
And – Ah! – Joy gives me strength! Who could defeat me?"

FOR WALTER KAUFMANN

Amid the wasteland, he
Created an alternative;
Proved poetry
Might live.

Refuting "the dung
The age demands
Be sung,"
His temple stands.

The age cries out
That he has missed
What it's all about!
Better yet – that he doesn't exist!

But the dung shall fade
In the sun –
Evaporate!
And his work live on.

WALDEN

Thoreau, in my mind,
Sits yet by the pond,
And thinks such thoughts
As would change humankind
By forging a better
Bond of oughts
Than the fetters
On those he's left behind.

He pushes beyond
The tangled knots
And the tired rot
That enslaves –

He finds the truth
Which frees and saves
Soul's youth.

ROMANTICISM'S BIRTH

To let the spirit break
Free from rules and make
Its own way
To whatever
Beauty it chooses to seek or take.

By its freedom, making seem
Art's toiling endeavor
Child's play
Or lover's dream.

ARENA (FIRST MOON LANDING)

The arena is silent –
Indifferent.
Nothing lives nor stirs –
Except –
What's this occurs?
A man has stepped –
Put his print –
Into the sand –
And,
Behind him, distant,
A race has learned to stand.

CHILD

Oh, child, I have known you!
Known your open eyes, your search, your fantasies
Of wild adventure, your shining peace,
Your easy, happy celebrating smile –
Did you think I would disown you?
Did you think I would somehow file
Your days away in a forgotten vault?
Who covers a statue that makes him exult?

Child! I know you! See you now!
See you dance here turning cartwheels on the floor!
See you twist and leap in overture –
To who knows what? What opera already forms
Itself in your mind? Tell! If time allow,
What are you going to do? What storms,
What stories, will you seek or start?
What is that star you carry for a heart?

My child, my self, we are yet one
In dancing spirit at least, and who's to thank
For that but you (or me) who never sank
So low that we actually drowned,
Resisting the lures of oblivion
With memories of the overture's sound –
Until we finally made our way to land,
Here to dance as I/you/we began.

Love Poems
1973 – 1974

Enright

MARSHA, THEY CANNOT SEE

Marsha, they cannot see.
Don't worry that we display
Our love too openly.

Beauty most obvious,
Most often they miss.

Children at the ocean shore
Know nothing of its motion's roar
At its proud center.

Ignorant, they enter
Up to their knees
And think they have seen all there is.

Don't fear. Though we bare it
Entirely, they won't begin to share it.

FLUSHED, LET US LIE

Flushed, let us lie
Together in perfection,
In post-orgasmic affection,
In satisfied sigh.

You feeling powerless, I
As God resting after creation.

PORCELAIN FIGURINE

Porcelain figurine caught in love's abandon,
Hair sweeping the air, hands the sky –
Outside it has snown – with snow as white
As the cumulus cross the blue.
The clouds will disperse – blow away
Into their million separate molecules.
The snow will melt – in a day and night
Come and vanished again.
The porcelain will sometime remain;
And love's abandon will go on
As long as snow, cloud, statue, blue
Or you
Are looked upon by me.
All the world's shifting forms
I see as symphony.

PROPOSAL

My destiny is at my feet,
And you are at my side.
Come live with me and be my love,
Come walk with me and be my bride.

When two souls such as ours meet,
They cannot part – become one life.
Come live with me and be my love,
Come walk with me and be my wife.

Poems
1974 – 1977

Enright

ROMANCE

A volume bound, no, not by what exists,
For hardly half could pass as history –
Even to a child, whose mind, still in the mists
Of ignorance and fancy, easily
Is taken in by those who would deceive.
No, none would think to literally believe
The stories which, enscriptured here, they find.
They know that what the artist would achieve
Is what could happen – heaven of the mind.

No, not Nirvana, not the Lethe's deep
Blind, drunken stupor of the mind's demise;
Romance has naught to do with death or sleep –
It is the art of life and open eyes!
Eyes open to the world and its potential,
Not dwelling on details of death or dearth,
But, through the nonsense, glimpsing the essential,
Beholding, through the worst of woe, the worth,
The joy, the power, of man's soul on earth.

A volume bound, by rules each must discover,
Apart from those the schools would now instill.
Rules known but to the maker and the lover:
The nature and the limits of the will.
Man's holy will! Oh, through the clouds of facts,
Shines clear the value of its sacred fire –
Repudiating temporary lacks,
Proclaiming now the force of that desire
Which ever lifts our being – higher – higher!

VISION
(After a painting of Sylvia Bokor's)

I see, in clear and vibrant hue,
A world hidden from your view.

Behold the yellow sunlight splash
Upon this bottle – hear the crash
Of sparkling color bursting from the glass!

But here – look at my painting of the scene.
Ah. You kneel. You know what I mean.

PHAETON EXPLAINS

It was no theft. The chariot
Was empty, and the coursers pulled
It without thought. My lariat
Flew out and put me in control.

There was no crash. The stories that
They later spread, of course, were lies
Designed to dull the glories that
So briefly flashed across the skies.

I shall return – upon the day
Men recognize my shining right
To wing an unobstructed way.
Till then, I'll only say: Good Night.

VOW

In the chapel
Of my soul
I kneel
And make a solemn vow:
Never any time – not now,
Nor in the future shall I bow
My head
Until I'm beaten – blasted – dead!
And even then – to die
With head held high!
This the soul of man demands.

Intransigence.

FOR MARILYN MONROE

Her lips a blessing of earthly bliss –
Her eyes all wide with happiness –
Her hair a halo – nothing less.
Her face eternal Christmas.

Her soul an anguished angel in a world
She cannot understand or learn to love.
But, dreaming of a better life,
She tosses off her pearls.

Marilyn, your beauty has
Departed, but its images
Hover still.
And ever will make me your lover.

TO THE STATUE OF LIBERTY

Torch –
Scorching the firmament,
Proclaiming your realm,
You stand at the helm
Of your battlements.
Liberty your text of law,
I pronounce your name with awe.

Lady of the Harbor, hear me!
Your land
Is dying, and your lesson
Is forgotten.
Statue, sear me!
Lend me your flame!
Let me be a weapon in your hand.

Grant to me the fire that cannot die,
So that your torch may ever scorch the sky!

PULSE

At my soul, the beat
Pulses yet.
Beneath the cool
Reflecting pools
Of reason
Is life.
Beyond contemplation
Is desire –
Raging, limitless fire –
Molded,
Controlled,
But, at last, the source –
Mind's driving force.

UNTIL NOW
(After Hertle's Painting)

Gleaming forms
Of stainless steel
He rearranges – and you feel
That what, till now, was dream
Is real.

A city by his single hand,
It does not merely seem –
It stands
As planned.

The sun begins to rise;
The forms
Reflect the warm
Of water's blue
And fill the skies.

What no one ever knew,
You see:
The mirrored towers of thought
Declare what can and ought
To be.

AFTER DALI'S CRUCIFIXION

He turns his golden, godlike head away,
In vain attempt to hide his pain, and, more,
To cast his own eyes far, and, hence, ignore
The agony he must endure this day.
The woman who is watching does not pray.
And yet, she worships, with a glance austere.
Her soul is steady. Neither dread nor fear
Can shake the awe which holds her in his sway.

Stretched out upon his cross, he hangs so high,
He seems to rise above his pain's existence –
No, not by height alone, but the insistence
Of his mind's might, which does not choose to die.
Overhead the darkness fills the sky,
But, tremblingly, a light shines in the distance.

AS WE DO NOT CHANGE

As we do not change
Except to grow stronger,
So love cannot change
Except to last longer.

We suffer, it's true,
And love suffers too,
But, just a we do,
Love perseveres.

No – never fear
That love will depart.
Now, as at start,
It inheres.

ENGAGEMENT RING

The clarity and fire
Of reason and desire
Frozen in a stone.
Take this ring of diamond and bright gold.
Hidden in its heart, it holds
All I am and own.

Wear it always, as a sign
That you are mine
And mine alone.

WEDDING CEREMONY

We stand, and know a moment in our lives
Which shall not be repeated, and we say
Words which shall follow us along our way;
Words which shall, as long as we, survive.

If there are none to stand beside us here
Just now, yet they surround us in their spirit;
Friends and heroes, souls by us held dear,
Worthy witnesses, all come to hear it.

Before the world today we sanctify
The sacred bond which has between us grown;
With rings of gold, with calm and steady eye.
We stamp each other for our very own.

Before the whole wide world we stand alone,
Proudly, arm in arm. And we march on.

With this ring I do thee wed.
With my heart and with my head
I take thee for my lawful wife;
To share with me whatever life
Is mine.

It shall be thine.

September, 1976

32

RETURN FROM ARUBA
(Coming back from honeymoon)

Desert nature, in her calms and storms,
Majestically reflects the moods of man.
The swirling sands, the undulating forms
Of sea and sky, the lay and rise of land,
All serve as mirror to meditation's eye.
Who can resist the long and languorous sigh
Of scented breezes in the embrace of night?
I can. For I return upon this flight
To New York City. Island paradise?
More so where I go than whence I come.
Aruba's lovely, but to my surprise,
I'm happy flying to my beehive home.
If man's reflective pleasure in deserted nature lurks,
What a greater measure must reside in his own works!

September, 1976

RAIN

Drip-drop,
Never stop.
Rain keeps beating on the old roof-top.

So I sit in meditation,
And my heart's own palpitation
Seems to match the rhythm
That the rain-drops carry with them.

Pour! Pour!
More! More!

Then cease.
Bring peace.

More Poems
1978 – 1995

I LOVE YOU, MARSHA

I love you, Marsha, for your mind,
I love you for your soul.
But I admire a plump behind,
And when it does a bump and grind,
I simply lose control.

VIGIL

When you sleep,
And I lie awake,
Holding you in my arms,
I pray:

Let me keep her
Out of harm's way.

A WRITER'S ART

What is a writer's art?
Like any savage, I attack,
Knife in hand, front or back —
It doesn't matter, let me stab
The blade into the chest — and grab
The beating heart.

ARISTOTLE

All the things that creep and crawl
Under the rocks,
He stares upon as stars –
In wonder.

No being above or below
His love of knowing.

ONE SUMMER DAY

One summer day,
Just before I turned seventeen,
After several sleepless nights,
I saw the light.

What can I say?
It was no vision, no single ray.
All I saw were sunny fields of grain,
Spread out forever across the plain.

Some sight.
And being alive was all right.

MICHIGAN DUNES

The wind sweeps the sand
away from the lake.

Thus stand the dunes.

In time, every grain
moves. The wind swoops down
and mountains of splendor
shift in the sun.

ROCK AND ROLL

Rock and roll is in my blood.
Love to thump and love to thud.
Rachmaninoff may raise the soul,
But only rock can make you roll.

It's a rhythm that grabs you
And pulls you along.
It's a pulsing that stabs you
And shoots through the song.

Beethoven, Mozart,
Chopin and Liszt –
May have higher art,
And would sorely be missed,
But without the Beatles
I wouldn't exist.

CHICAGO

The level freedom of the open plain
Extends, extends, extends.
The fields of waving grain
Threaten to never end.

Until, at last, the yawning lake,
Blue grey, swallows the green of land
And stretches on without a break.

Where lese but there to take a stand
And build a tower without top?
Between those two forevers,
The only way to go was up.

PHILOSOPHY AND POETRY

Ironic turns of mind
Combined
Into a mask of common sense –

This is my defense.
My crime
Is rhyme.

BEFORE CHRISTMAS

The longest night has come at last.
The sky is dark and overcast.
The howling wind kicks up the snow.
Outside is no place to go.

And yet, the wise men let us know
That from now on the nights will all
Be shorter, and the days more long,
That slowly the sun shall shine more strong,
And turn the tide of fall.

Winter, be a time of hope!
Of course on dreary days we mope,
But seeing the slight increase of light,
Let us celebrate after this longest night
With yule log fire and boughs of green
Hung up to remind us that we mean
To witness again the coming of spring –
That blossoming blaze that always brings
Good things beyond imagining.

VALENTINE'S DAY

Enclosed: one heart.
Handle with care.
I'd rather you didn't
Bend, fold or tear.

C.O.D. charges:
A kiss and a hug.
And maybe a little
Roll on the rug.

1980

FIRSTBORN

Because we live,
We give
You birth.

What is love
Unless we share it?

Inherit
The earth.

LENNON

Who said, "We are more popular than Jesus,"
Now dead like Jesus, murdered senselessly.

Who sang, "Bang Bang went Maxwell's Silver Hammer,"
Nailed dead. And silence black hangs overhead.

Whose words brought half the world to its feet
And set us jumping in a holy frenzy –

Now lain before us, slain by rotten envy.
The beat goes on. But our hearts miss a beat.

December, 1980

BIRTH BALLAD

It was just about midnight
And up out of bed
Jumped Marsha. "I've got
A contraction," she said.

They kept coming on,
And I timed them with care.
They lasted ten minutes,
Which didn't seem fair.

By one they were coming
Five minutes apart.
So I called up the doctor
And he said to start.

So I shaved and I dressed
And was ready to go,
But Marsha threw up
And held up the show.

Then we got in the car
And I stepped on the gas
With the perfect excuse
For speeding – at last!

The rest – it all blurs,
But after six hours
Out came a boy!
Sweet joy! He was ours!

May, 1981

BABY DEAR

Baby dear,
the charm of you
disarmingly
commands a smile.

Despite your loud
alarms,
I love to hold you
in my arms.

September, 1981

VALHALLA
(For Ayn Rand)

They laid her in the ground,
The geese flew overhead,
And in a "V" they swooped around,
Then shot away.

As if to say,
She isn't really dead.
Her spirit's merely fled
To where the heroes play.

OUT IN THE WEST

Out in the west
Where the land is wide
And a hundred miles
Is just a ride,

Where water is scarce
And the clouds are few,
You somehow change
Your point of view.

The roads are so clear
That nothing is far.
Horizons are near
Wherever you are.

The sun goes down,
The stars come out,
And shine in glory
All about.

NOELLE

I hold in my arms
A person so small
That she's almost – just almost
Quite no one at all!

Someday is so far,
But soon – very soon,
What now seems an eighth note
Will play like a tune.

January, 1984

RECANTATION

Galileo, having confessed
The error of his ways,
And having promised
To follow true doctrine
All his remaining days,
Was released by the Inquisition.

Considering afresh his position,
He stared at the ground and declared,
"IT STANDS QUITE STILL!
IT STANDS QUITE STILL!
AS THE CHURCH COMMANDS!
AS THE BIBLE PROVES!"

He lifted his head
And quietly said,
"Nevertheless, it moves."

MISTLETOE

As the Druids did of old,
Let us go and watch the sky.
In the dead of winter's cold,
Mistletoe hangs green on high.

At the top of oaks stripped bare,
It clings to life without compare.
Thus we cling to those we love,
When mistletoe is seen above.

HALLOWEEN

Put on a mask of scary glee
And dance around the fire with me.

The summer's gone, the autumn's come,
But that's no reason to be glum.

The leaves shall burn and rise in flames
And nobody shall know our names.

Then each to each may trick or treat,
As whirling smiles turn sour or sweet.

At midnight's stroke, all draw their breaths –
For now false faces face their deaths.

Off with the masks! Away with the elves!
We come back to life as our favorite selves!

And only the Reaper is left feeling Grim,
As we merrily twirl away from him!

September, 1984

A DOZEN YEARS

A dozen years,
You've been my dearest.
Is it so many?

My only regret
Is that there were any
Days in my life
Before we met.

Be my wife
A hundred years yet.

February, 1985

I KNOW YOU WELL

I know you well,
And I can tell,
That no one else
Can cast a spell
So sweetly as
You do – Noelle.

MEETING YOU

Glorious and sweet,
Victorious defeat.
I won your love
And lost my heart
To you.

Delirious delight,
Too serious to fight.
I climbed so high
And fell so hard
For you.

FOR A DAUGHTER THREATENED BY ILLNESS

Daughter, you are my nightmare and my dream.
My dream of sweet brightness like sunlight cascading
On fields of white daisies that laugh at each beam,
My nightmare of all the sun suddenly fading,
And all that brightness gone – forever gone.

Oh, do not die! Outlive me thirty years!
And when I die, please bury all my fears
With me, beneath the ground. But take my love
And toss it upward, in the air, above,
To light your way when my own day is done.

July, 1989

ROBIE HOUSE

Amid the gothic grey
University gargoyles –

Where beauty was banished
So that no sight could sway
The intellect from ever greater toils,

Frank Lloyd Wright
Came to play.

To build a house with windows wide and bright
With flowing rooms that beckon and invite
With jewel-like shapes that dazzle and delight.

And on that spot,
That blessed lot,
All dark spirits vanish.

STARBOUND

Some day when there are men on other planets,
Not there to visit, there to live and breed,
They will look back upon this earth and scan its
Blue cloudiness, and ask: where was the need?

To kill each other over scraps of land,
When space was lying open all the while,
Beckoning, glistening to the wandering mind,
Waiting for a race to match its scale.

As walls come tumbling down around the world,
As tyrants fall, and throngs of people stare
Upon new possibilities unfurled,
Their eyes turn, too, to what awaits Out There.

As freedom spreads, and puts an end to wars,
The time will be at hand to settle stars.

MARATHON

Into the distance
Run at full speed.
Something bright glistens
Something you need.

Over the hill
And beyond the next dale.
Where there's a will
There's no way to fail.

September, 1992

ECONOMIC SUMMIT

Savages with Ph.D.'s
and various other advanced degrees
gather together, proclaiming the need
for government spending to hasten the speed
of economic growth.

Alas, it's hard to have both.

The biggest growth they have in mind
is of the more malignant kind –
strange and strangling rules and regs
designed to tangle up the legs
of all who run for cash.

I fear a minor crash.

1993

HEALTH CARE

So you want a right to health care?
I'm glad to hear it, friend.
We've bundled up a bunch of laws
To help you meet that end.
A friendly little system, where,
No matter what your state,
We'll slice your paycheck, just because
It makes us feel so great.

And if you're feeling poorly, well,
We'll put you on the list
Of those who need a doctor bad...
And if you still exist
A year from now – why – what the hell
We'll let you see a nurse
Who'll tell you what it was you had
And why it's gotten worse.

We'd let you see a doc, except
We're kind of understaffed.
We told them what we'd pay them now
And most of them just laughed.
We threatened them, we begged, we wept,
And told them they must stay.
But strangely – we're not sure just how –
They all have slipped away.

Worry not! We'll fix you yet!
We're training new recruits.
Fellows much too bright to go on
Sweeping streets and shining boots.
They're doing great at school – you bet!
We're grading on the curve!
Brains they're slightly low on,
But we believe they'll SERVE!

THERE IS NO JUSTICE IN YOUR DEATH

There is no justice in your death,
  no purpose in your pain.
But in your life, in every breath,
  there was a world of gain.

To us you were a treasure bright
  shining all a-glitter,
Filling us with rare delight
  dissolving all the bitter.

November 1993

WHENEVER I THINK OF HER

Whenever I think of her
I first will picture her smile.
There was something about it
that was utterly beguiling.

I think it was the trust
she gave when she felt you cared.
She really did believe
that life is best when shared.

She wanted – oh, so much –
to be a mother someday,
to feel the tender touch
of her own bouncing baby.

Now, it will not be.
That hope is torn from my soul.
But in her hour, she
lived her part with a heart that was full.

November 1993

DECEMBER 24, 1993

Noelle, Noelle, my darling daughter, dead,
Not forty days, but Christmas Eve has come,
And everywhere I go I hear it sung:
Noel, Noel, oh joyous sing, Noel.

Noelle, Noelle, when you were born, we said
That you embodied Christmas joy so well,
No other name would do. But now, instead,
It echoes sadly, like a funeral knell.

The stockings and the wreaths have all been hung,
And soon the drummer boy will beat his drum,
In celebration of a child whose birth
Brought warmth and love to all who live on earth.

While she lies silent, cold beneath the ground,
Whose laughter was this long night's gayest sound.

PRAYER TO WISDOM

Grey-eyed Goddess, your unwavering gaze
has been my source of strength through all my years.
When the world around me stirs my fears
and spins me downward in a daunted daze,
when panic's fog consumes the sun's bright rays,
and clogs my eyes with cloudy stinging tears,
I think of you and then confusion clears –
The wind of Wisdom blows away the haze.

Your wind does not blow easy. It blows hard.
No zephyr calm and breezy, flowing past
in gentle comfort. Instead, a freezing blast
of arctic clarity, an icy guard
against delusion's warmth. This way is barred
to those who cannot face cold truth at last.
But, for those who dare, the view is vast.
What can hide from Wisdom's high regard?

Clinging to that windswept peak, I see
spread out before me, wondrous, intricate,
the workings of the world, together fit
in ways I never would have guessed to be,
and each new understanding is a key
unlocking doors behind which treasures sit,
but warning as to where the viper's pit
may lie in wait for feet that run too free.

Oh, Wisdom! give me strength! for I must face
a world without my daughter. She has died
in innocence and misery. We tried
so hard, but failed, and now her rightful place
is empty. Vanished is the vibrant grace.
Banished is her banter from my side.
Vanquished am I. Goddess, be my guide.
Help me to see past our last embrace.

This loss, so near, looms large and blocks my view,
a great black hole that swallows all my light,
and only on the edges of my sight
can I make out the world's normal hue.
How terrible that tragedies imbue
surrounding scenes with shades of death and night
plunging planets whole into the plight
of one small child who had to say adieu.

Help me to see that there is beauty still
within the world, to see that life goes on,
and on, and on, until each breaking dawn
begins to whisper to me that I will
some day wake up without this aching chill,
this disbelieving grief that she is gone.
Help me to wake some morning with a yawn
and greet the sun's smile without feeling ill.

Wisdom, I know your ways are often slow.
Give me the patience to endure this while,
to let the hands of time turn on the dial,
spinning the wheels that make the seasons flow.
The day will come – I pray – I hope – I know –
When I'll look back this way without denial,
and without joy, but with a saddened smile,
behold her whole life bathed in a golden glow.

And on that day, oh Goddess, let me not
forget you, you who gravely pulled me through
these worst of times. Oh, let me think of you
together with her, in a sunny spot –
and she will bring you daisies in a pot,
and you will smile at her, and softly, too,
your great grey eyes will turn a shade of blue
to grasp the grace she brought to her short lot.

BEST EFFORT

She always used to ask me if I'd won
when I came home from running some hard race,
and I would tell her no, but I'd had fun —
that would put some light back in her face.

I jog now to her grave, for exercise,
or so I say — I need a place to go.
When I reach it, tears fill up my eyes,
and out my mouth there bursts a moan of woe.

Kneeling in the January snow,
across the letters of her name, I trace
my fingers. I know that she is done
with caring over running. I rise.

At school she used to run. She took a prize
last year because her effort was the best.
Cursed by illness, but with spirit blessed.
Sleep, my darling, you have earned your rest.

_____

January 1994

HER COUSIN JACK

Her cousin Jack,
who lost a tooth,
said: Since Noelle's
an angel now,
I bet her job
for God must be
to come back as
the tooth fairy,
'cuz that's a job
she would have liked
very, VERY much!

And if I thought
he spoke the truth
then every night
I'd pull a tooth
from my own mouth
and stick it there
beneath my pillow –
and lie awake
to catch a glimpse
or feel the touch
of that sweet shining face.

1994

PERSEPHONE

Spring bounds upon us in a burst of green,
Shooting new leaves upward from the ground,
Budding in the night with force unseen,
Unfolding in the day without a sound,
To take us unawares by sudden view
Of naked color – yellow, pink and blue –
Swaying in an ecstasy of hue.

Sweet princess, Spring, escaped from out the grip
Of Winter's icy hands, how you have grown!
How full the lips where brazen bees will sip.
How tall the stalks where tiny seeds were sown.
Reaching skyward, sunward, with a thirst
For light and love. And with a cloudy burst
Of pollen, all the world is immersed.

Gone, washed away, is the grime and the grey,
Flushed from the day by the flowers' wild spray.
The frigid, rigid death of low degrees
Is brought to breath again – each warming breeze
Revives us more. And grief within my heart
Begins, slowly, to thaw. In every part
Persists the longing for a newborn start.

April, 1994

HAUNTED WORLD

Some say the world is an empty place
With bits of matter sparsely interspersed.
But everywhere I look, I see the face
Of one I loved – of one for whom I thirst.
I say, instead, the world is immersed
In tears and kisses, bonds and interactions.
Its matter fusing into nova bursts,
Exploding by repulsions and attractions.

The cross-linked cells that fire in the brain
Reverberate and trace the world's events,
Echoing with vibrations that contain
The energetic pulsing of each sense.
Look up at night – a galaxy immense
Sprawls out – and yet is gathered in a glance
As separate waves of light converge – condense –
Into one image of the vast expanse.

The world is haunted – haunted by our minds –
Hunting its face, according to our goals,
Sorting, importing, storing away our finds
Safe within the mapping of our souls.
From high and holy places – to the holes
That drop to regions sulfurous and dread,
The world is a scripture, and its scrolls
Unroll within the temples of the head.

And everywhere we turn, we see the traces
Of what has gone, and hints of what will be,
Whether in our old familiar places,
Or in some strange new land across the sea.
Her memory still lives – inside of me,
And still I see, in others, something of
The beauty and the gracefulness that she
Left within this world – by our love.